Mountain Top Musing II

Along the Path of
The Warrior Poet's Heart
Tenderness Awaits

Written By

Pete McKechnie

*Melanie and Melissa.
You never know. Perhaps a
signed copy of my books will
be worth something, someday.
Be Well.*

Design and Layout by

Nancy Smaroff

Previous book:

Mountain Top Musing (Vol I)
A Reluctant Poet's Glimpse
Into His Own Heart

Watch:

"Pete McKechnie" on YouTube

Follow:

Pete's work on Facebook at
"Mountain Top Muse"

Contact info:

mountaintopmuse@gmail.com

Acknowledgements

I owe a gift of gratitude to someone named Marylou.
I use the word 'someone' because I don't know who
or where she is, only that she, with a handful of words,
pointed me in this direction.

I never wanted to be a poet. I wanted to write short
fiction. I've never seen myself as a writer or a poet, but
for the last twenty-three years I have seen myself as
someone who just happens to write poetry. This has
shifted for me very recently, and I have finally owned
that yes, I am a poet.

Many years ago I took a creative writing class at the
University of Maryland, College Park. One of the stories
I submitted for the class was absolutely shredded by the
instructor. I had made a very conscious decision to write
that story in a way people simply don't talk or think
anymore. I knew there was a risk within the style I chose.
I didn't expect it to get directly thrown into a meat grinder
by the instructor. After that class, it became clear that no
one else expected that either. I am not sure how many
came up to me after, and said a variation of 'I have no
idea what that was all about.'

One person in particular came up to me after, and after
saying her variation of that phrase added 'I think you
should write poetry.' I smiled and thanked her. As we
walked our separate ways I thought 'You're crazy.
I don't want to be a poet.'

Around the time I decided I was a poet, perhaps twenty-seven years later, a friend of mine brought up a different short story I had written. I didn't actually remember even showing it to him. Later that day, while searching through my old writings, I found a copy of the story that had been torn to pieces so many years ago. It was one with lots of notes on it, notes that I never read at the time. At the time, after the critique, I had just put all that stuff away. One of the notes read —

"Marylou wants you to write Victorian love poems for her."

Coincidence.

Not Victorian, or specifically love, but here are some of the poems written while I was busy not being a poet.

Thanks Marylou

* * * *

So many friends and family have played a critical role in me becoming a Poet. Of course, Nancy Smaroff once again played a critical role, taking on the role of editor and formatter. I may have ended up publishing a book at some point, but to say that Nancy was a critical part of Mountain Top Muse is a huge understatement.

Contents

x

One Path

There will come a time
Where the path I have walked
And the path I will walk
Will be one and the same.
There will come a time
Both are defined as one.

This time will come
At the end of the path,
When there are
No more steps to take.

Until then,
If I embrace and love this path,
I will understand
That all the steps I have taken
Are the foundation,
And all those left for me to take
Are the mystery
Into which to dive.

Steps Taken

If my steps forward
Are taken
Only to escape my past,
I will have missed the mark.

And if my steps forward
Are hindered
By an inability to let go,
I will have as well.

When my path forward
Flows naturally from my past,
And lessons learned
Direct my choices,
I will not only
Fail to miss my mark,
It will have no choice
But to leave my mark
On this world.

Gift of Feeling

I was there then.
I am here now.
I will be there tomorrow.
What matters, I wonder?
Because where I was then
Felt overwhelming,
And what I feel now
Does as well.

Where I will be tomorrow
Feels un-touchable.
When I understand this, I see
That it is not so much
That I understand what I feel,
But that I allow myself
The gift of feeling.

And that it is the gift
Of feeling where I was,
And where I am,
And where I will become
That allows me to know
Who I am truly meant to be.

Ultimately

Ultimately,
The challenges we meet today
Will not feel much like a challenge.
Ultimately,
We will understand
That what we face today
Will become the fodder
That creates our reality.

Ultimately,
We will understand
That that which happens now
Is of far lesser significance
Than the ways in which
We choose to handle it.

Ultimately,
We will see
That we are active participants
In our own reality,
And hopefully, ultimately,
We will choose a
Higher Calling.

To Have Lived

It is impossible to tell
What will be left for me,
Or of me,
At the culmination
Of my experience of life.

It is possible that the coffers
Will be full,
Overflowing with possessions
Too numerous to count.
It is also possible
That within this life
I will lose it all.
It is possible
That everything I own
Will be taken from me,
And that the coffers will be
Stripped bare.

I have, I hope,
Come to terms with this possibility.
I have, I hope,
Come to see the truth.
I can die with it all,
Or die with nothing,
Either way,
As long as I die
With Love,
And Faith,
I will have lived.

Greeting the Day

The sun will rise tomorrow.
This I know.
It will rise, and offer me a day.
What will become of this day,
What will be offered,
Is beyond my understanding.

But it is not beyond my control,
Or my choice,
To greet this day open-hearted.
It is not beyond my choice
To allow what will become
To guide me into the next day.

So, let me wake each day
With the understanding
That while I do not know
What is in store for me,
I do know
That the way in which
I greet each day
Will be the greatest factor
In how I choose to live it.

Longing Prevents

What do I long for,
I wonder?
What would make me whole?
What would bring me peace,
And make
The troubles in my life
Worthwhile?

As I ponder this
I begin to understand
That longing for anything
Is an act
That will prevent me
From feeling whole,
And that peace is a gift
I can only give myself.

So my troubles are not
Placed on me by the world,
I place them on myself,
And in order to avoid this
I must accept responsibility
For my own happiness,
And my ability to feel whole.

Perception

It is within my power
To choose how to live this life.
It is within my power
To keep an open heart,
Or to allow my insecurities
To shut me down, close me.

I have chosen both
At different times.
I have blamed others.
But at the end of this day
It is up to me
If it was a good day,
Or bad.

It is up to me
To see the clouds
Or the sun,
And it is up to me
To understand
That my life
Will never be greater
Than my perception
Will allow.

Releasing Agenda

I can see the truth
As the colored leaves fall.
I can see that the giving in
Is inevitable.

I can taste the truth
In a moment of sensation,
Knowing that the passage
Of that moment
Is inevitable.

I can hear the beauty
Of the song,
Knowing as the rhythm fades.
Inevitability reigns.

I can feel the possibility,
But as my grasp weakens,
It escapes my fingertips,
In an end I know will come.

And while the scent is in the air,
I realize that my senses
have miss-led me
To a moment
A personal agenda has desired,
And the truth is
My desires will never be
As great as my truth.
So, let me let go of my senses,
My agenda,
And allow myself, simply,
To accept.

My Soul, My Self

Come to me.

Why?

Because I want you to.

And what will you do,
When I come to you?

Well, I will sit.

You will sit?

Yes. Come to me.

Why?

Because I need you to.

And what do you need?

Just to become.

Just to become?

Yes

I do not understand.

Why?

You will just sit, become?

Yes, when you come to me,
I will just sit, and become.
I will simply sit in my truth,
And become my essence.

By coming to me,
You will have honored
That which is most true of me,
And that which you
have the greatest difficulty,
honoring in yourself.

Come to me.

Just Listen

I am calling you, you know.

Why can't I hear you?
I feel the need for
Your voice.
I need you.

Then listen.

I am.
Speak louder.

No, I will not speak louder.
Listen more clearly.

And how do I do that?
I beg for your words
And hear nothing.
I cry for you
And your silence
deadens my soul.

Well, have you witnessed
A sunrise?
Has the scent of a flower
Touched your nose?
Have you seen
The dance of the bees
On the flower of a clover?

Well, yes, I have.

Then you have heard
My voice.

I don't understand.

Of course you don't,
Because you don't really
Want to know me.

Yes, I really do.

Then wake up, dear child
Because I am calling you.
I am calling everything
That is real in you
With everything that
Is real of me.

What is real of you?

Love.
And when you choose
To understand,
You will know
That what is real of me
Has no choice
But to be real of you.

Then, you will hear
My call.

Giving Way To Light

Darkness has no choice
But to give birth to light.
We might awaken
To the dawn
In unfamiliar territory.
The previous day's sunset
Might leave us feeling
As if the light has been taken
From our life.

Darkness has no choice,
And as it gives birth
Eternally to light
A new day will dawn.

Each day,
This is the light,
This is the gift,
In which we shall live.

Letting Go

Holding on is an act
That both clings to the past
And attempts to
Direct the future.
It binds us
To days gone by
And directs us
To days yet to be,
All the while
Preventing us from living
This one day,
Present to its gifts.

Letting go is an act
That neither clings to the past,
Nor attempts to
Direct the future.
It frees us from
Days gone by
And allows
The days yet to be
To remain a mystery,
So that we can live
This one day,
Present to its gifts.

The Meaning of Life

What meaning do I have
In this life?
How is it that my existence
Means much of anything?
None, perhaps,
In the grand scheme of things.

My life is, and will be,
A speck of dust
Blown into the wind,
But as this speck blows,
Its meaningless existence
Dancing in the breeze,
What will it have done?

Well, given a choice
In this meaningless existence,
And lasting only a moment
In time,
I will hope my little speck of dust
LOVED,
And that will be
Meaning enough for me.

Come To Me

Come to me.

I hear these words,
Whispered gently
On the breeze.
I feel the pull,
And strike off
On my journey.

Come to me.

I hear these words again,
Whispered gently
On the breeze.
And as the journey
Draws me ever forward
I find myself lost
Within this wilderness.

Come to me.

I no longer hear these words,
Rather they resonate
Within my soul.
And I begin to understand
That the gentle breeze
Which has whispered
Into my heart
Is my own,
And it has guided me here.
It has guided me
Back to myself.

Choosing the Legacy

When I wonder
What I might choose
To do with my life,
The canvas seems open,
Endless.
It seems that
I could do anything,
And there is great truth
And responsibility
With this understanding.

I can choose to control,
Or destroy.
I can choose to fight.
I can choose
To force a destiny
On others
In order to suit
My own desires.
I can, also, choose
To let go.
I can choose to create,
And allow destiny
To actualize the path
That suits not only me,
But, also, the paths
Of all those around me.

So, when I wonder about choice,
Let me both understand
That I have it,
And that the legacy
Of my life
Will depend upon
What I choose
To do with it.

Waiting

I can hear the silence.
I can feel the desire
Within my heart
As connection is sought.
I can feel an emptiness,
A void,
And my heart aches.

I also know
That this silence
Will soon transform,
And what my heart
Aches for now
Will be followed
By the connections
That are most deeply
Important to my soul.

Surrender

Surrender is an act of will.
It is an act that undermines
The reality our ego
Has so passionately built.

Surrender is also
An act of purpose,
One that will allow our ego
To transcend the reality
Built by our mind
Which no longer feeds
The nature of our heart.

Surrender is an act of will,
And the only act
That will free the Heart
From the convention
The ego clings to,
In its attempt
To guide the path
Of life.

Breathe

Breathe,
I remind myself.
This is merely a lesson.
This is simply
A moment of experience,
And it doesn't
Define or describe
My life.
It will not only pass,
It will become a guidepost
Along my journey.

Breathe,
I remind myself.
Allow what is,
So that what will be
Can become.

Breathe.

Faith and Heart

There are times
When my faith weakens,
And my doubts
Find themselves emboldened.
I cherish these moments.
Honestly,
I almost look forward to them.

As difficult as they may be to transcend,
To understand,
They illuminate the path
Of understanding.
They show me
That without these trials,
Though they create within me
The thought to question
My faith,
I will never understand
Just how deeply my faith
Resides in my heart,
And how strongly
My heart
Can guide my life.

Here and Now

Right here, right now,
My life is simple.
I take in one breath at a time.
I take in the sunrise,
The sunset.
I know nothing
Except the now.

When I step away
From this presence,
And allow worries
Of the future
To cloud my moments,
I accept complexity into my life,
My heart.
I allow the future
To dull these moments,
And shroud them with
Uncertainty.

I allow a possibility
To obscure my reality,
And thus risk losing
The gifts
My present moment has to offer.

Created Turbulence

I have been looking for myself.
Trying to find
A pathway to my heart.

I have found this endeavor
To be a challenge.
I find that the distractions
Of life
Muddy the waters,
Creating turbulence and discord.

I find the path overgrown,
Impassable.

But when I still myself,
I begin to understand
That the muddy waters
Of distraction
Are nothing more
Than my own attempt
To obstruct
The pathway of my heart.

When I still myself,
I understand
That it is turbulence
Of my own creation
Which leaves me with the feeling
That I was ever even lost.

The Soul's Truth

It is true
That for some of us,
Expression seems a risk.
Our dreams, we fear,
Might seem frivolous,
Or be scorned.

In truth,
We have no choice
But to express.
The purpose of a life
Is to allow a soul
To declare,
And it is not the soul
Which fears
Its expression might seem frivolous.
It is the mind,
Through the filters of this life,
Which fears these things,
And attempts to dictate
The soul's ability to express.

Just speak
That which comes from the heart,
And dream that which is held most dear,
And know
That the only true consequence
Of this expression
Is the soul's ability
To be whole.

Choice, Destiny

It matters not
Whether what we perceive as choice
Is in fact merely a matter
Of destiny.

While our destiny
Might be out of our control,
It is the choices
Which bring us there
That embody
Either acceptance or resistance,
And allow us
To either flow with the path
That leads us to ourselves,
Or struggle along the way.

In each instance,
Ultimately,
We will find ourselves
Exactly
Where we were meant to be.

The Open Door

There is a door, open,
Before me.
All I have to do
Is find the courage
To enter.

Yet, I hesitate,
I hold back,
And while I will not let
The door close,
I will not allow myself
To walk through.

I could call this patience,
Or temperance.
I could call it prudence.
But this is denial,
Because walking through
That door
Is exactly
What my soul
Is drawn to do.

Why Wait?

What is it about
The prospect of dying
That creates within us
The desire to live?

How can we not
Embrace this gift?
How can we not
Choose to live every moment,
Until we are faced
With the reality
That these moments
Might be limited?

Let me awaken each morning
And relish the gift of dawn,
Living each day
As if it were my last.

Only then will I understand,
That life cannot offer me anything
Other than this moment
In the sun.

What I Leave Behind

It is clear
That each of my actions
Has an impact upon this world.
That my actions resonate deeply
Through the universe,
Even if they seem to me
Inane, simple, mundane.

When I ask myself,
What wake I would like to leave,
How heavily I would want
To rock the boats of others
With the waves
Created by my actions,
I would be missing the point.

It is not the response
Others might have
To my passing
That I am responsible for.
It is the way I choose to pass,
Because even an act of love
Can be met with discord,
Just as an act of hatred
Can be smiled upon
By one who resonates
With that destructive force.

So, I will not concern myself
With the effects of my actions;
I will concern myself
With the nature of them.
I will let myself understand
That no matter what
My actions leave behind,
And no matter that
I can understand it,
If I act in love,
My passing, ultimately,
Will be a gift to all.

Beyond The Veil

It can be easy,
In this busy, modern world,
To fail to look
Beneath the surface,
And witness only
The pale views of life
Our busyness allows.

It is more challenging,
In this busy, modern world,
To take the time to look
Beyond the simple veil,
And find the substance
That lies in waiting
To fill our soul.

Let this path not be easy,
And let my busyness subside,
Allowing me to take the time
To look beneath the surface,
And witness only
The full view of life
And the essence that lies within.

One Life

I can dwell
On those things
My life lacks,
Or explore
The gifts
My life gives.

I can dwell
On the pain,
Or dance with
The joy.
I can choose
To see the empty spaces,
Or choose
To live in the fullness.

Ultimately,
It is the same
Life I observe,
And it is the perspective
With which I observe it
That creates
The reality in which I live.

Ego Or Heart?

When I choose to express,
I should ask myself:
What voice am I choosing?
What is the intent
Behind my words?

I should ask myself
If my ego has something
To gain from my words,
Or if it is my heart
Whose beating
Depends on them.

I should ask myself
If ego is directing the discourse,
Or if I am allowing,
In that moment,
My heart to direct
The substance
Of the words that flow.

And I should understand
That no matter what
The words might be,
If it is my ego
that wishes to speak them
I should pause, hesitate.

If it is my heart
That is the source,
I should speak them now,
And clearly.

Our Truth

In any given moment,
We are offered the opportunity
To choose fear and hate
Over love and compassion.
It is not always a choice
Which comes easily.
It is not always a choice
That appears to serve
Or ensure,
The survival
Of our ego.

When we look deeply
Into the nature of our souls,
We will see
That the choice of
Love and Compassion,
Though sometimes
More challenging to pursue,
Most clearly defines
The true nature
Of our Truth.

Sacred Honor

I can honor you,
I can honor them.
In moments of clarity,
I realize
I can look around me
And honor all I see.

For some reason, however,
I cannot seem to honor myself.
All the worth
I see around me
Will not translate
Into Worth
I can see in myself.

I know this
To be incongruous
With reality.
May I know
That the value
I can find in others
Is no greater
Than the value
I should honor in myself.

Our Destiny

Life is often described
As a battle,
A struggle,
A circumstance
To be overcome,
Conquered.
Life can be seen
As a series of hardships
That with hard work
And diligence,
We will transcend.

The truth is
That the struggle
Of life
Has nothing to do
With circumstances
Experienced,
And that the greatest strife
Is caused
When we hold on,
Tightly,
To our own desires
As Creation drags us
Kicking and screaming
To our destiny.

Speaking Our Wisdom

We may not understand it,
But when we choose to speak,
We choose an audience
To hear our words.
We choose our words carefully,
In order that the ears
We wish to hear our message
Will be peaked, and open,
To what we have to say.

What we do not understand
Is that it is easy
To seek an audience,
It is easy to speak our wisdom
To others,
And if they should not hear it,
Walk away with assurance
That if our wisdom had fallen
On open ears,
Our words would have hit their mark.

What we do not understand
Is that often,
The being most in need
Of our own wisdom
Is our true Self,
And when we choose to speak,
More often than not,
It is us
Who needs
This wisdom.

Silence Before Words

In most cases,
We will do
What we have been taught.
We will attempt
To use words
Woven carefully together
To communicate
That which lies deepest
In our souls.

However, we often miss
In our aim
When we attempt
To express truth
With words.
In reality,
Our essence can most easily
Be expressed in silence,
And our spirit is expressed
Most clearly
Through presence.

I would hope
That each time I desire
To express myself with words,
I first sit in silence,
Long enough to be sure
That the words I choose to speak
Reflect the true nature
Of what my soul is desiring
To express.

A Devastating Life

Let me live a life
That will leave devastation
In its wake.
One that
will leave a sense
Of emptiness
That overwhelms the senses
And takes the breath
From every soul
My life has had the privilege
With which to intertwine,
When the day of my passing comes.

Let me not live that life
In order for those lost souls
To be lost.
Rather
That my very existence
Filled them to the point
That my passing leaves them
So empty,
That the only desire
That could live on in their heart
Is the desire that no other soul
Would feel that desperation.
That each beat of their heart
Would live only
To fill the existence
Of others.

Ego and Humility

There is no humility in ego,
But there is plenty of ego
In humility.

If you wonder
About the validity of this,
Ask yourself,
Do you need humility to see yourself
As above all others?
Of course, the answer is no.

But to be truly humble,
Do you have to be strong enough
To see yourself
As you truly are,
As neither more, nor less
Important than any other?

Yes.

Let Me Love, Creator

Let me love, Creator.
Allow me the grace
To hope,
To dream,
To fantasize.

Show me how to smile,
To laugh,
To cry.
Gift me with wisdom,
Inspiration.

Confuse me by allowing me
To witness
The darkness that seems
To contradict your light.
Gift me with the pain
I might need
In order to allow myself to grow,
And the joy I might feel
When I come to understand
The path I have chosen to walk.

Most of all, Creator,
Whatever You may
Have in mind for my life,
I ask for the greatest gift.

Whatever comes, Creator,
Never let me hate.
Hatred is
The one thing
That can keep me
From connecting to You.

On Loving All

There is ease in the notion
Of loving those closest to me.
Be they my children,
My family,
My friends,
How could I not,
When those closest to me
Are an integral part
Of my reality,
Myself?

What is more challenging
Is the ability
To redefine the notion
Of my Children,
My Family,
My Friends,
And to understand that
For me to be an integral part of the world,
There is no part of the world
That is not integral to me.

So, perhaps I should not long
To love those closest to me.
That is simply the nature of life.

I should long to love all,
For in reality,
The only way not to love something
Is to not love an aspect
Of myself.

Heart's Path

There is no chance
That I could think a path
That is greater than
My heart would imagine.

The trick, I know,
Is not to allow my mind
To decide,
For my heart,
Which path to follow.

Should I do that,
I would allow my mind
To conjure
A life less fulfilling
Than my heart is
Meant to live.

Heart Over Mind

It is the mind that expects.
It is the mind which
Paints pictures
Of the way the future
Might look.
The soul, the heart,
Are incapable of this act.
They are only capable
Of being the painting,
In all its glory or pain,
In the moment
That exists right now.

Should I grant myself one wish,
I would hope
That I remember this,
And let go of expectations
In order that my heart,
My soul,
Can simply represent
The image created
On this world
In each moment
Of my life.

Leaving My Mark

I wonder, at times,
How it is possible
For me to leave my mark on this world.
How I could ever live up to
The brilliant minds,
The brilliant souls,
The brilliant hearts,
Who are dotted throughout history.
How could I ever achieve
Such wondrous things
That these truly inspired people
Have come to be remembered for?

There are other times,
I allow my own light to shine,
And fully understand.
While the mark of others
Might seem extraordinary,
None of them could have
Stroked the pen
Which will leave my mark
On the world,
Any more
Than I could stroke theirs.

There is no greater gift
I can offer this world
Than to live the life
I was given to live.

Easy Or Simple?

Synonymous as they are,
The words easy and simple
Offer vastly dichotomous
Experiences of life.

An easy life
Is built on the expectations
Of the world in which
One is born,
Dependent on the resources
Required by that life.

A simple life,
Regardless of the society
Into which we are born,
Requires only the ability
To follow the heart
Which beats for the moment,
And for the soul's expression
Of its truth in this life.

I will not ask
For an easy life.
To gain that life
I would have to fight,
Tooth and nail,
To achieve status
In the society
Into which I was born.

I will ask for a simple life,
Because all I would have to do
To achieve that
Is to allow my heart and soul
To express
Their truth.

Choosing The Choice

Choice is the illusion
That allows us to believe
We have control
Of our destiny.
It is the vehicle
Of our own deception
Which we use
To excuse our willingness
To force our will on our truth.

And yet, choice is critical
In our attempt to express.
For in each of us
Is a destiny,
And it is our life's mission
To choose to embrace it, or not.

So, let me understand
That it is my destiny
To choose the life
That was preordained
And chosen for me,
And though I have the ability
To strive for an alternate life,
I will be happiest
When I 'choose' the life
That has been chosen
For me.

Allowing Life

I can live for other
Or I can live for myself.
In the end,
It matters not.
In the end,
There is one thing I will never know,
And that is simply what,
Ultimately,
Is best for other,
And what,
Ultimately,
Is best for myself.

I think,
Ultimately,
That I should not concern myself
With what might be best for others.
I think,
Ultimately,
That I should not worry what
Might be best for me.
In the end,
Simply,
Allow my life to unfold,
Without expectation,
And allow myself to be.

Painting My Life

If I knew I could paint my life,
And was given the chance to do so,
What should I look to paint?
How should I paint the picture
That will become my life, my love?

Should I look forward
And attempt to guess
The picture I might draw?
Should I attempt to control the outcome
By painting what I think I want
Into a picture
That decides my path?
Or should I wait, patiently,
And discover
How my life might unfold without control,
And see what life's destiny
Draws for me?

I will put my brush aside,
In trust of
The Designer's brush,
And wait.

What is drawn for me
Is what I will live.

Anticipation

I find myself,
At times,
Sitting in anticipation,
My thoughts focused
On what is about to become
Or wondering
What could come to pass
In the years that lie ahead.

I find
That this anticipation,
While fodder for my mind,
Can also be a poison
To my soul.

I find it serves naught
Other than
To pull me out of this moment,
Even when, perhaps,
This moment
Is the one
I had been anticipating
Through the years.

Writing From The Future

In this moment,
I am not who I was
In the past.

In this moment,
I am not what I will be
In the future.

I am simply who I am,
In this moment.

Yet I know
That what has transpired
In my past
Has helped create
My current reality,
Even if
The person I was then
Is not the person I present now.

I also know,
That what I am willing
To see in myself now
Can limit
Or create
My future.

Should I withhold
My expression in this moment,
I might curtail the truth
Of the person who will,
Years from now,
Sit back and write
This poem.

Embracing Powerlessness

To be disempowered
Is an act others
Might perpetrate on me,
And should I choose to look deeply,
I will see
That without me allowing it,
This act will not be.

To be powerless is different.
This is a state
I will only find myself in
When I understand
That while I might guide my life,
I do not direct it.

I would ask to be powerless,
Not disempowered.
I would ask that a greater power
Steer my choices,
Rather than accept
That this world within which I reside
Dictate the path of my life.

I would choose to understand
That to be powerless
Is the gift
That allows me to embrace
What will become,
And that if I allow myself
To be disempowered
It would be to choose
Never to be whole.

Resisting Mystery

There is a mystery to life,
An unfolding,
That can neither be seen
Nor stopped.
After this opening,
Should we truly delve
Into the mystery,
We will understand
That this is all we have ever been,
And is exactly what we have resisted.

This is the place
To where I have come,
And I can both perceive the mystery
And understand my role
In resistance.
I find myself ready, rested,
And finally willing to embrace
The gifts which have waited,
Patiently,
To be accepted
By my heart.

Control, Or Not?

When I look to see
What aspects of my world
I can control,
Ultimately, I will have
To understand
That my response
To circumstance
Is the only power
I might have.

I cannot dictate
The actions of others,
Or find the ability
To manage
The response
That might become
Of my experience.

So I will, and I must,
Follow my own truth,
And allow
The response of others
To be theirs.

In a singular moment,
The truth that is seen
Will be dependent
On the eyes which see.

And should this be my life,
It is my own eyes
Whose perception
I should trust.

Silent Words

There are times
Words cannot express
The depth of feeling,
Knowing.

In these times,
Nothing will suffice
Save the silence
Of true connection.
Only the heart
Understands these times.

Only the soul
Will resonate
In the depths of this bliss,
As silence itself
Becomes the greatest
Form of communication.

Reflections of Beauty

Is it possible, truly,
To witness beauty
In this world
If there is not
A reflection of beauty in myself?
I would suggest not.

What I perceive
Will not take hold of my heart
Unless the resonance of truth
Abides.
This is true, also,
With ugliness,
And should I choose to witness
Only the darkness of this world,
It is only because
I am choosing to resonate
With those dark spaces
In myself.

So it is my choice, now,
To decide
What I would most like to witness.
I can choose to allow my
Essence to resonate
Most clearly with beauty,
Or allow it to resonate
Most clearly with the darkness.
It is with this choice,
I will determine
My perception of this world.

Awakening

There is great risk
In awakening.
In order to become
That which we are meant
To be,
We have to understand
That what we see ourselves
To be
Is the greatest illusion.

This is the cliff
We are all presented with
At some point in our lives.
And while many
Who choose not to leap
Will lead a seemingly happy life,
It is only those
Who fall into the abyss
Who will find the true nature
Of their soul.

The Apple

To reach for the Apple,
They say
Is to reach for
The forbidden fruit.
It is to open one's self
To sin.

They, also, call it
The Fruit of the Knowledge
Of Good and Evil.

Perhaps we should understand
That without the choice
To partake of the Apple
Our choices are limited.

Without the option
To choose evil,
A choice for good
Carries no weight.
Without an understanding
Of darkness
The gift of light fades.

Give me the Apple.
Let me partake.
Let me choose,
Tomorrow,
The light of dawn.

We Do What We Are Told

I will walk past you,
Dying in the gutter.
I will ignore your pain,
And revel in my joy

Why would I do this?
I do it
Because you do not
Understand my God.
I do it
Because you are not
Attracted to the gender
That I believe you should be.

I will do it
Because the rich tell me to.
I will do it
Because they tell me that
My path to freedom
Depends on my willingness
To walk past you in the gutter.

So I will walk past you,
Dying in the gutter.
Not because I don't care,
And not because I don't want
To stop and help.
I will do it because
Those to whom I have given my power
Are walking past you,
And I don't have the strength,
Or heart,
To think for myself.

So I will walk past you,
In the gutter,
And if there is a glimmer
Of hope
For my soul,
I ask of you
To have the wisdom
To smile at me
When my turn comes to die
In the street.

It Is Not Shaming, Right?

It's not shaming, right,
When I look at a guy
In a convenience store,
Whose belly is many
Inches past,
And bellow
His belt,
And think God,
I don't want to look like that?

I didn't speak,
And he didn't know
My thoughts,
So that's not shaming, right?

It's not shaming, right,
When I witness
A person clearly
Less well-off than I,
And I think, thank God,
That is not me?

I don't speak,
They don't know,
So that's not shaming, right?

It's not shaming, right,
When I see a person
Who is different,
And think,
I am better than you?

I don't speak.
They don't know.
So that can't be shaming, right?

But I might be
Shaming myself,
And it's not shaming, right,
When each of them looked at me
And thought... ?

Silencing Myself

There is nothing
In this world
That has more power
To silence me
Than myself.

No knife to my throat
Or gun to my head
Can quiet my voice,
Unless I allow it.
Only I can silence
My voice.

Only I can still my words.
Perhaps I will die
For my words,
Or suffer rejection,
And the hatred
Of our times.
But it will be my choice,
And it will rest on my soul
If I choose to withhold my words.

But I will not have been silenced,
I will have silenced myself.

Born and raised in Maryland, just outside of Washington, DC and having spent six years living in Holland and England, Pete McKechnie's resting place now is the Potomac Highlands of West Virginia. He lives in the mountains, but they are not his mountaintop.

He spent many years teaching meditation workshops and working with developmentally disadvantaged children. As a builder of custom homes, he realized his love for the feel and texture of wood. These were some of the steps to his mountaintop, but not the peak. In Pete's words, "With different passions and goals, we all climb different mountains. In the end, what matters most is that we reach the Mountain Top. When I choose not to live in the valley and find the grace to live on the mountaintop, expression through poetry is my peak."